SERIES TITLES

PREHISTORY	I	XIII	SETTLING THE AMERICAS
MESOPOTAMIA AND THE BIBLE LANDS	II	XIV	ASIAN AND AFRICAN EMPIRES
ANCIENT EGYPT AND GREECE	III	XV	THE INDUSTRIAL REVOLUTION
THE ROMAN WORLD	IV	XVI	ENLIGHTENMENT AND REVOLUTION
ASIAN CIVILIZATIONS	V	XVII	NATIONALISM AND THE ROMANTIC MOVEMENT
AMERICAS AND THE PACIFIC	VI	XVIII	THE AGE OF EMPIRE
EARLY MEDIEVAL TIMES	VII	XIX	NORTH AMERICA: EXPANSION, CIVIL WAR, AND EMERGENCE
BEYOND EUROPE	VIII	XX	TURN OF THE CENTURY AND THE GREAT WAR
LATE MEDIEVAL EUROPE	IX	XXI	VERSAILLES TO WORLD WAR II
RENAISSANCE EUROPE	X	XXII	1945 TO THE COLD WAR
VOYAGES OF DISCOVERY	XI	XXIII	1991 TO THE 21ST CENTURY
BIRTH OF MODERN NATIONS	XII	XXIV	ISSUES TODAY

SETTLING THE AMERICAS
was created and produced by McRae Books Srl
Via del Salviatino 1 — 50016 — Fiesole (Florence)
Italy
info@mcraebooks.com
www.mcraebooks.com

Publishers: Anne McRae, Marco Nardi
Series Editor: Anne McRae
Author: Neil Morris
Main Illustrations: M. Gaudenzi pp. 10–11, 22–23,
26–27; Alessandro Menchi pp. 8–9; MM
comunicazione (M. Cappon, M. Favilli, G. Sbragi, C.
Scutti) pp. 14–15, 16–17, 20–21, 30–31
Other Illustrations: Studio Stalio (Alessandro Cantucci,
Fabiano Fabbrucci), Lorenzo Cecchi

Maps: M. Paola Baldanzi
Photography: Bridgeman Art Library, London: pp.
13tl, 28–29c, 32–33c, 36–37, 42–43b, 44–45c
Foto Scala, Florence: p. 19b, 34–35t
Granger: p. 7b
Art Director: Marco Nardi
Layouts: Starry Dog Books Ltd
Project Editor: Loredana Agosta
Research: Loredana Agosta
Repro: Litocolor, Florence

Consultant:
Dr. Ronald Fritze is a historian of early modern
Europe and England. He is the author of *New Worlds:
The Great Voyages of Discovery* (Sutton/Praeger, 2003).
He appeared on the History Channel series *The
Conquest of America* and is a member of the Society
for the History of Discoveries.

Library of Congress Cataloging-in-Publication Data

Settling the Americas
 ISBN 9788860981752

2009923563

Printed and bound in Malaysia.

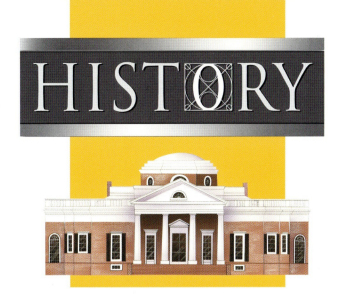

HIST✺RY

Settling the Americas

Neil Morris

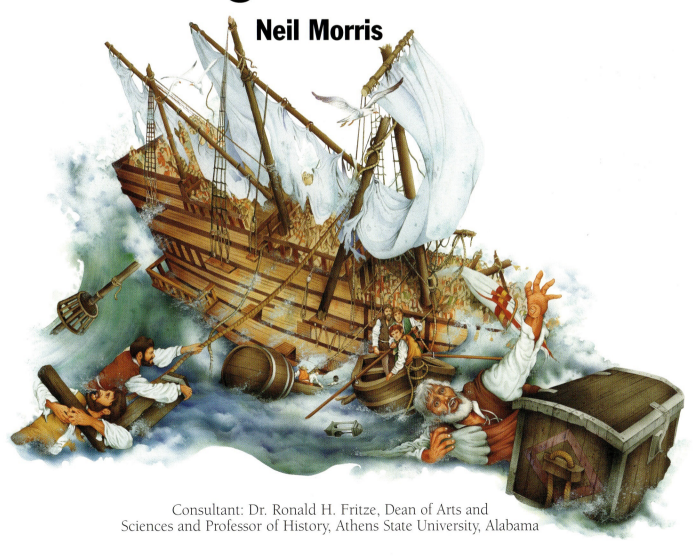

Consultant: Dr. Ronald H. Fritze, Dean of Arts and
Sciences and Professor of History, Athens State University, Alabama

Zak
BOOKS

Contents

5 Introduction

6 Colonization

8 The Spanish in North and Central America

10 The Spanish in South America

12 Bourbon Reforms

14 The Portuguese in Brazil

16 The Age of Piracy

18 The British, Dutch, and French in Latin America

20 Trade and Industry

22 The British in North America

24 The Dutch and the Swedish in North America

26 The French and Louisiana

28 The Thirteen Colonies

30 The Colonial Home

32 The American Revolution

34 The United States

36 Religion in the New World

38 Colonial Art and Architecture

40 Early Canadian Settlements

42 The Fight for Canada

44 Under British Rule

46 Glossary

47 Index

A European portrait of the Native American princess Pocahontas, who sailed from Virginia to England in 1616.

TIMELINE

	1500	1535	1570	1605
CENTRAL AMERICA		The Council of the Indies is set up to control colonies from Spain. The Viceroyalty of New Spain is established.	Acapulco is founded on the Pacific coast. After Spain colonizes the Philippines in 1565, galleons begin sailing across the Pacific from the Far East, loaded with exotic goods.	The viceroy of New Spain drains Lake Texcoco and the Valley of Mexico to extend the land that can be built on.
SOUTH AMERICA		Francisco Pizarro founds Lima. First permanent Portuguese settlements are founded in Brazil. The Viceroyalty of Peru is established.		
CARIBBEAN ISLANDS		The Audiencia of Santo Domingo is set up in Hispaniola.		Dutch West India Company is founded.
EARLY NORTH AMERICA (USA)				The British establish Jamestown. The Dutch establish New Netherland. The Pilgrims found Plymouth.
THE UNITED STATES				
CANADA				Pierre du Gua and Samuel de Champlain found a settlement on an island in the St. Croix River. Quebec is founded.

Introduction

Following the great voyages of exploration made by Columbus and others, Europeans sailed across the Atlantic to colonize the two continents that the explorers had discovered. They found that this "New World" offered many treasures, from silver and brazilwood in the south, to valuable furs in the north. The Spanish dominated Central and South America and by the 18th century they had established four viceroyalties. The Portuguese took coastal Brazil and quickly expanded inland. In the north, the British and French vied for control of Canada. The 13 British colonies of North America came together, created a constitution, and by 1783 had won a revolutionary war to gain full independence. This book tells the story of European settlement in the Americas, from the beginning of the 16th to the end of the 18th century. During that time many of the colonies became self-governing provinces of their mother country, while the United States became a separate nation.

Native American slaves working on a Spanish sugar plantation in Latin America.

The Sanctuary of Bom Jesus in Congonhas, Brazil, was built in the colonial Baroque style in the 18th century. The church was designed by Aleijadinho (see page 38).

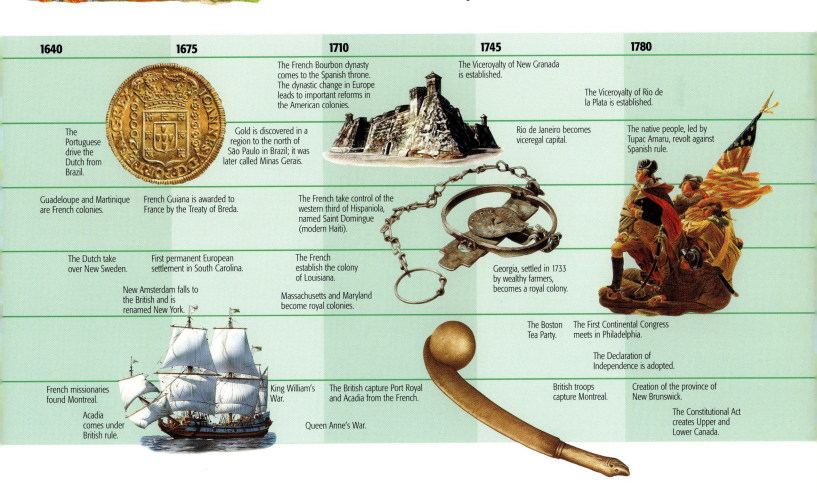

1640	1675	1710	1745	1780

The French Bourbon dynasty comes to the Spanish throne. The dynastic change in Europe leads to important reforms in the American colonies.

The Viceroyalty of New Granada is established.

The Viceroyalty of Rio de la Plata is established.

The Portuguese drive the Dutch from Brazil.

Gold is discovered in a region to the north of São Paulo in Brazil; it was later called Minas Gerais.

Rio de Janeiro becomes viceregal capital.

The native people, led by Tupac Amaru, revolt against Spanish rule.

Guadeloupe and Martinique are French colonies.

French Guiana is awarded to France by the Treaty of Breda.

The French take control of the western third of Hispaniola, named Saint Domingue (modern Haiti).

The Dutch take over New Sweden.

First permanent European settlement in South Carolina.

The French establish the colony of Louisiana.

Georgia, settled in 1733 by wealthy farmers, becomes a royal colony.

New Amsterdam falls to the British and is renamed New York.

Massachusetts and Maryland become royal colonies.

The Boston Tea Party.

The First Continental Congress meets in Philadelphia.

The Declaration of Independence is adopted.

French missionaries found Montreal.

King William's War.

The British capture Port Royal and Acadia from the French.

British troops capture Montreal.

Creation of the province of New Brunswick.

Acadia comes under British rule.

Queen Anne's War.

The Constitutional Act creates Upper and Lower Canada.

Colonization

European colonists sailed to the Americas for a variety of reasons. Once there, they reacted and developed in different ways, according to local conditions and the cooperation or opposition they encountered from the local population. Colonization was devastating for native peoples, many of whom died of diseases carried by the Europeans. The newcomers set up forms of government and trade that benefited themselves and their European homelands.

Left: This vase shows the three peoples of colonial Latin America—Native American, European, and African.

European Powers

The major European powers—Spain, Portugal, England, France, and the Netherlands—saw the Americas as an opportunity to maintain or even increase their individual share of growing world trade. There was inevitably great rivalry between ambitious merchants and colonists on the American continents, as they fought for control over goods and trade routes. This reflected the political and religious struggles that were going on between the nations in Europe.

Above: Like many other European monarchs, George III of Great Britain and Ireland (reigned 1760–1820) encouraged tough policies toward the American colonies.

Native Peoples

The Spanish conquest of Central and South America destroyed the native cultures, including the magnificent Aztec and Inca civilizations. The colonists who followed the conquerors ruled by a system of forced labor. The situation was different in North America, where smaller tribes of Native Americans had to learn quickly to adapt to the ways of the new settlers. Some fought each other as well as the European invaders, as their lands disappeared and their way of life changed.

Right: A Spanish colonial portrait of Manco Cupac, the legendary first Inca emperor. Descendants of the Inca in Peru were forced to work for Spanish colonists.

In Search of Freedom

People emigrated to the American colonies for many different reasons. Some, such as the Puritan Pilgrims, went in search of religious freedom. European merchants were more interested in the economic benefits of trade, and many did not stay in the colonies for long. They needed workers, some of whom were happy to accept free passage for the prospect of a new life.

Growing Colonies

Throughout the Americas, local conditions shaped the way in which colonies developed and European colonists adapted to their new way of life there. Climate, geography, and natural resources varied enormously between the tropics of Central America and South America and the colder regions of the northern British colonies and Canada. European settlers had to adapt quickly to these local conditions in order to survive.

Left: This is how Plymouth colony looked seven years after it was founded in 1620 (see page 23).

Left: This 1698 certificate of indenture promises free passage and maintenance to a 15-year-old Englishman in return for four years' work and servitude on a Virginia plantation.

Below: Pennsylvania Quakers. Many left Europe to avoid religious persecution.

The Mayflower Compact

Colonists decided on their own forms of government. In 1620, before coming ashore on the American coast, the Pilgrims aboard the *Mayflower* drew up and signed an agreement. They decided to join together as a "civil body politic" and obey the laws to be drawn up for their colony by those chosen by common consent.

Below: Forty-one men signed the Mayflower Compact off Cape Cod on November 11, 1620.

NORTH AND CENTRAL AMERICA

1511
The Audiencia of Santo Domingo is set up in Hispaniola.

1524
The Council of the Indies is set up to control colonies from Spain.

1535
The Viceroyalty of New Spain is established.

1542
The New Laws of the Indies try to end abuses of the encomienda system.

1607
Luis de Velasco, son of the second viceroy of New Spain, begins the drainage of Lake Texcoco.

1629–34
Floods hit Mexico City, forcing people to move to Puebla; Mexico City is rebuilt in the Baroque style.

The Spanish in North and Central America

Spanish colonial territories in the Americas grew during the 15-year rule of the first viceroy of New Spain. This expansion led to the successful exploitation of the gold and silver that the Spanish had been so keen to find. The colonies were run under a system called *encomienda*, by which the Spanish crown granted colonists the right to demand tribute in gold or labor from native inhabitants. At the same time colonists were responsible for protecting native peoples and instructing them in Christianity, though many did not take this responsibility seriously.

A 1649 map of the Spanish walled city of Santo Domingo, on the coast of Hispaniola.

Portrait of Antonio de Mendoza (c.1490–1552), first viceroy of New Spain and third viceroy of Peru.

Pacific Trade

Acapulco was founded on a deep natural harbor on the Pacific coast of New Spain in 1550. After Spain colonized the Philippines in 1565, so-called Manila galleons began sailing across the Pacific from the Far East, loaded with Chinese silk, porcelain, precious stones, and other exotic goods. The ships unloaded at Acapulco, and goods were taken overland to the Gulf of Mexico for further shipment to Europe. The Manila galleons loaded up with Mexican silver for the return voyage.

This enamelled earthenware jar from Mexico shows a Chinese influence.

In 1638 the Manila galleon Nuestra Señora de la Concepcion foundered in bad weather on its voyage to Acapulco. The ship hit a reef off the Mariana Islands, most of the 400 people on board drowned, and its precious cargo was lost.

Treasure Fleets

From the 1560s, fleets of galleons sailed from Spain to the American colonies. They loaded up with gold, silver, copper, tobacco, and other precious treasure, before leaving the Mexican port of Veracruz for the return voyage across the Atlantic, protected by warships. They often faced terrible storms, as well as danger from pirates, and many ships were lost.

Spanish Colonial Government

Each of the Spanish viceroyalties, or colonial provinces, was run on behalf of the king of Spain by a viceroy. This senior official acted as governor, supervisor of the colonial treasury, captain-general of the military, and vice-patron of the Church. The viceroy was also president of the *audiencias*, regional courts and administrative centers that also served as executive councils. As a third tier of the hierarchy, each region had a number of local parishes and mayors.

The Council of the Indies

The Council of the Indies, which was resident in Spain, was made up of six to ten councillors appointed by the king. The Council ran the American viceroyalties on behalf of the monarch, preparing and issuing all laws relating to the colonies, approving expenditure by officials, and acting as an appeal court. Among the councillors were lawyers, clergymen, geographers, mathematicians, and secretaries.

This illustration of San José del Cabo, on the Pacific coast of Baja California, Mexico, dates from 1762. A Spanish galleon is seen arriving from the Philippines.

THE VICEROYALTY OF NEW SPAIN C. 1650

- Audiencia of Santo Domingo, 1511
- Audiencia of Mexico, 1529
- Audiencia of Guatemala, 1544
- Audiencia of Nueva Galicia, 1549

ATLANTIC OCEAN

Gulf of Mexico

GUADALAJARA

MEXICO

SANTO DOMINGO

Caribbean Sea

GUATEMALA

PACIFIC OCEAN

New Spain and its Regions

The Viceroyalty of New Spain was divided into four audiencias (judicial districts), shown on the map with their founding dates and capitals. The courts of the audiencias had authority to hear complaints against captains general or even the viceroy. They were also supposed to safeguard the rights of local native people, setting aside two days a week to hear cases involving locals.

The Spanish in South America

Portrait of Diego de Almagro (1475–1538).

The early colonial period in South America was complicated by disagreements between the conquistadors. Ten years after the Spaniards occupied the former Inca capital of Cuzco, the viceroyalty of Peru was established as the second such colony in the Americas. Disputes continued, and the first viceroy, Blasco Núñez Vela, was killed in battle by supporters of Gonzalo Pizarro, brother of Francisco. By 1600 the region had seen 14 viceroys, but by that time Peru was considered the most valuable Spanish possession in the Americas.

From Conquistadors to Rulers

The Spanish conquistador Diego de Almagro had helped Francisco Pizarro conquer the Inca empire, and the two friends became joint captains general in the new colony. After they fell out over the running of the city of Cuzco, Pizarro's forces won the day and executed Almagro. In 1541, Pizarro was killed by followers of Almagro's son, who was then defeated in battle by soldiers of the Spanish king. Two years later, the first official viceroy took office.

This silver-gilt enamelled monstrance (a container for the consecrated Host) was made in 1646 by a Spanish craftsman in Lima.

SOUTH AMERICA

1535
Francisco Pizarro founds Lima.

1536
Unsuccessful Native American rebellion led by Manco Capac.

1539
La Plata (modern Sucre, in Bolivia) is founded on the site of a Charcas Native American village.

1543
The Viceroyalty of Peru is established.

1568
A Spanish mint (for silver coins) is established in Lima.

1569–81
Francisco de Toledo is one of the most able viceroys of Peru.

1578
The port of Callao, near Lima, is pillaged by Sir Francis Drake.

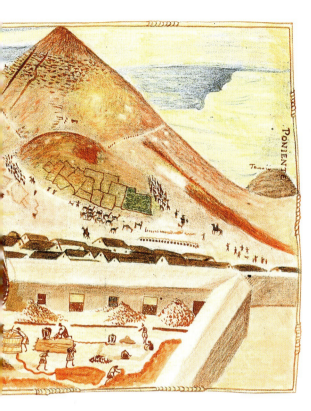

The silver mine was dug into Cerro Rico ("rich hill"), above Potosí.

Silver City

The discovery of silver in the Andes Mountains of present-day Bolivia in 1545 led to the foundation of the city of Potosí. Large-scale excavation began at a mine near the city, which lay to the southwest of La Plata. Silver bullion was soon being sent to Spain, and people flocked to Potosí. By 1650 the population of the city, which lies at 13,000 feet (3,976 m) above sea level, had reached about 160,000.

Lima

The city of Lima was founded in 1535 by Francisco Pizarro. It was built on the banks of the Rio Rimac, just 8 miles (13 km) inland from the Pacific coast. Two years later Pizarro established the port of Callao on the coast, and the port and city formed a major distribution point for gold and silver. Lima became a focal point for Spanish expansion, and by the 17th century it was the center of Spanish government in South America. It is the capital and largest city of modern Peru.

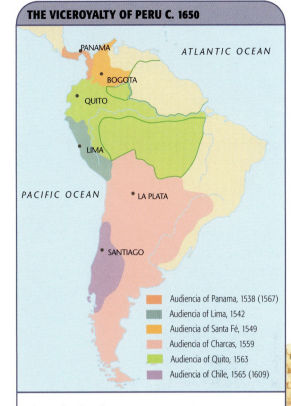

THE VICEROYALTY OF PERU C. 1650

PANAMA
ATLANTIC OCEAN
BOGOTÁ
QUITO
LIMA
PACIFIC OCEAN
LA PLATA
SANTIAGO

Audiencia of Panama, 1538 (1567)
Audiencia of Lima, 1542
Audiencia of Santa Fé, 1549
Audiencia of Charcas, 1559
Audiencia of Quito, 1563
Audiencia of Chile, 1565 (1609)

The Audiencias of Peru
The Viceroyalty of Peru was divided into six audiencias, shown on the map with their founding dates and capitals. The territory bordered New Spain to the northwest of the Panamá region and to the northeast of Santa Fé. From 1559 the huge territory of Charcas covered modern Bolivia and included parts of present-day Argentina, Chile, Peru, and Paraguay.

Native American workers and llamas carried silver-rich ore down from the mine to the growing city of Potosí.

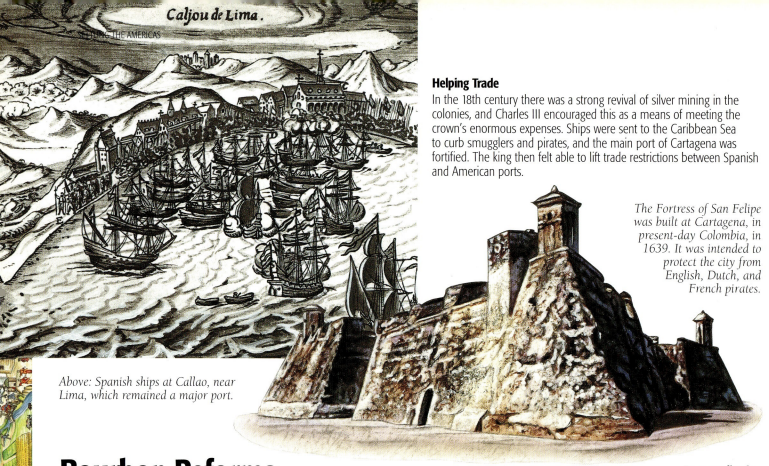

Caljou de Lima.

Above: Spanish ships at Callao, near Lima, which remained a major port.

Helping Trade

In the 18th century there was a strong revival of silver mining in the colonies, and Charles III encouraged this as a means of meeting the crown's enormous expenses. Ships were sent to the Caribbean Sea to curb smugglers and pirates, and the main port of Cartagena was fortified. The king then felt able to lift trade restrictions between Spanish and American ports.

The Fortress of San Felipe was built at Cartagena, in present-day Colombia, in 1639. It was intended to protect the city from English, Dutch, and French pirates.

Bourbon Reforms

In 1700 the French Bourbon dynasty came to the Spanish throne, replacing the Habsburgs. This dynastic change in Europe led to important reforms in the American colonies, especially during the reign of Charles III (1759–88). Peru was split into three viceroyalties, as the Spanish looked to keep control of trade and stop incursions by pirates in the Caribbean and by the Portuguese from their territory of Brazil. At the same time a new level of provincial administration was added.

Decentralization

As well as creating a fourth American viceroyalty, Charles III further decentralized the colonies by introducing a new level of provincial governors, called *intendentes* (intendants). They were able to relieve overburdened viceroys of some of their duties, and were especially helpful with revenue collection. Many intendants were capable administrators, who also promoted education and culture.

SPANISH VICEROYALITIES 1784

ATLANTIC OCEAN

MEXICO CITY

HAVANA

CARTAGENA

BOGOTA

LIMA

PACIFIC OCEAN

BUENOS AIRES

Reorganization

The New Granada Viceroyalty was created under Philip V, with its capital at Santa Fé (modern Bogotá, Colombia). The Viceroyalty of Rio de la Plata, created by Charles III, had its capital at Buenos Aires (Argentina). This growing city took over much of the shipment of silver to Spain. The creation of the new southern province was also intended to stop Portuguese expansion from their colony of Brazil.

■ Viceroyalty of New Spain

■ Viceroyalty of New Granada

■ Viceroyalty of Peru

■ Viceroyalty of Rio della Plata

Portrait of Charles III by Ginés Andrés de Aguirre (1727–1800), who was a successful painter at the royal court in Madrid and then in Mexico City.

BOURBON REFORMS

1700–46
Reign of Philip V, the first Bourbon king of Spain.

1740
The Viceroyalty of New Granada is permanently established (after temporary existence 1717–24).

1762
British expeditionary force holds Havana for six months.

1767
The Jesuit order is expelled from Spain and Spanish America.

1776
The Viceroyalty of Rio de la Plata is established.

1783
Spain regains control of Florida (having ceded it to England in 1763).

1789
Free trade is allowed between all qualified Spanish ports and the American provinces.

Below: Detail of a painting of a Spaniard with his Native American wife and their mestiza child by the 18th-century Mexican artist Miguel Cabrera (1695–1768).

Above: This 18th-century painting shows a busy market in the main square of Mexico City, New Spain.

Supporters of Tupac Amaru wore feather headbands, like this one, in honor of their Inca ancestors.

Revolt

Peruvian peasants attempted to rebel against tough Spanish rule in 1780. They were led by a local chief who changed his name to Tupac Amaru, after the last Inca ruler to resist colonization. The revolutionaries executed a Spanish administrator on charges of cruelty, but in 1781 Tupac Amaru was captured. He and his family were executed, and the uprising was put down in the following year.

Life in Spanish America

The people who benefited most from the economic advances were the descendants of Spanish immigrants who were merchants and landowners. Born in America, they were known as Creoles, and many had large commercial and mining interests. Some of the officials working for the new intendants treated the native population badly. In the middle socially were the mestizos, who were mixed descendants of Spaniards and Native Americans.

Slaving Expeditions

From the 1620s, colonial entrepreneurs began organizing slave-hunting expeditions into the Brazilian interior. The journeys were undertaken by adventurers called *bandeirantes*, who raided native villages and Jesuit missions. Most bandeirantes were from the São Paulo region, and many were part Native American. In one early expedition, a group raided 21 villages and captured about 2,500 slaves.

Bandeirantes cut their way through the rainforest, with slaves literally in tow.

The Captaincy System

In 1533, a year after the first colonies had been established by the Portuguese admiral Martim Afonso de Sousa, King João III divided the Brazilian coastline into 15 parallel strips. These strips of land, some of which were larger than Portugal itself, were hereditary fiefs known as captaincies. They were granted to individuals, who were allowed to develop their land economically, to charge taxes to colonists, and to enslave native people. The captaincy system lasted for more than 200 years.

Portrait of Martim Afonso de Sousa (c.1500–64).

The Portuguese in Brazil

The Portuguese settlement of Brazil was based on trade and commercial interests (see pages 20–21). Settlers exploited the colony's brazilwood, then grew sugar cane and mined the gold and diamonds that were plentiful in the region. The coastal area was divided by the Portuguese king into captaincies, where individuals were encouraged to use their entrepreneurial skills to exploit the natural resources—including the native population—to the full. Slave-hunters led the drive to explore and conquer the interior of Brazil.

Expanding Boundaries

São Paulo bandeirantes headed north toward the Amazon River, west to present-day Paraguay, and south toward the Plate River. In the process they expanded the boundaries of the Portuguese colony. Jesuit missionaries protested, but were forced to move ahead of the slave hunters. The map shows the expansion of Portuguese territory.

🟧 Portuguese lands by 1600	🟧 Gold
🟧 Portuguese lands by 1750	🟩 Diamonds
🟪 Portuguese frontier lands	→ Slaving expeditions

THE EXPANSION OF BRAZIL

ATLANTIC OCEAN

MANAUS

BAHIA

SAO VICENTE
RIO DE JANEIRO
SAO PAULO

Mining for Gold

In 1690 *bandeirantes* discovered gold to the north of São Paulo, in a region that was later called Minas Gerais ("general mines"). The discovery led to an enormous gold rush, as more people emigrated from Portugal and existing colonists swarmed down from the northeast of Brazil. Most prospectors used slaves to pan for gold in streams; pits and excavations were less common. In 1729 diamonds were also discovered in the region, adding to its importance.

These gold coins were minted at Minas Gerais in 1726.

Peoples of Brazil

From about 1550, the owners of sugar plantations began to use more black slave labor imported from Africa. They replaced native slave workers on many large estates. A mixture of Europeans, Native Americans, and Africans made up the Brazilian population, and many children were born to a combination of the three groups. In the 18th century, foreign minister Marques de Pombal (1699–1782) encouraged the social mingling of native peoples and Portuguese.

Above: A Portuguese nobleman is carried in luxury, illustrating the master-servant relationship.

BRAZIL

1532
First permanent Portuguese settlements are founded in Brazil.

1554
São Paulo is founded by Portuguese Jesuit priests.

1580–1640
Portugal is under Spanish rule.

1660
Amazonian settlement of Manaus is founded.

1700
A royal despatch denounces the barbarous treatment of slaves.

1709
Minas Gerais becomes a separate captaincy.

1759
Jesuits are expelled from Portugal and Brazil.

1763
Rio de Janeiro becomes viceregal capital.

This astronomical compendium, made by the English instrument-maker Humphrey Cole in 1569, included a sundial and an engraved list of latitudes. It may have belonged to Drake.

Buccaneers

The term buccaneer comes from the French *boucan*, a grill for smoking dried meat for sailors to eat at sea. The first buccaneers were a group of French outlaws in Hispaniola who began raiding passing ships in the early 17th century. They were later joined by English and Dutch sea adventurers, who terrorized Spanish ships from bases in Tortuga and Jamaica.

Anne Bonny and Mary Read dressed as men to sail as pirates with Jack Rackham.

Blackbeard's larger ship tries to chase down a sloop. Queen Anne's Revenge captured 18 ships in 7 months.

The Age of Piracy

Large treasure fleets regularly left Cartagena and other ports along the Spanish Main (the Central and South American coast of the Caribbean Sea). Along with less protected Spanish galleons and the ports themselves, the ships were vulnerable to attack by pirates. Many of these sea adventurers operated outside any law, while others were privateers, authorized by their monarch to attack ships of an enemy country. Gold and silver from the Spanish colonies formed their greatest prize.

The Golden Age

The period from about 1690 to 1730 has been called the "golden age" of piracy. As well as terrorizing the Spanish Main, pirates set up in the Bahamas to attack the Atlantic seaboard. Among the causes for this dramatic increase in piracy were the large number of seamen who were unemployed or very poorly paid for their work. Naval action, especially by the British royal fleet, finally put an end to the period.

Portrait of Christopher Myngs by Sir Peter Lely (1618–80).

Flintlock pistols were popular pirate weapons.

The Pirate Ship

Though pirates such as Blackbeard and Bartholomew Roberts liked to sail in big, well-armed ships, most preferred smaller craft. One of the most popular pirate ships was the sloop, which normally had a mainsail and a foresail and could carry up to 75 men. It was a highly maneuvrable craft with a shallow draught, which made it easy to sail and hide in creeks and lagoons.

The Queen's Sea Dogs

Seeing Catholic Spain as an enemy, Elizabeth I of England (reigned 1558–1603) gave Protestant Dutch privateers safe harbour. She then encouraged English captains, who were sometimes known as "sea rovers" or "sea dogs," to raid Spanish ships. The queen sponsored her privateers, who were given licences called "letters of marque," and she shared in their spoils.

Blackbeard

Blackbeard was the nickname of Edward Teach, an English seaman who sailed first as a privateer. In 1717 he captured a French transport ship, which he armed with 40 guns and renamed *Queen Anne's Revenge*. Blackbeard terrorized the Virginia and Carolina coasts of North America, until he was killed by a lieutenant of the Royal Navy. Divers discovered the remains of his ship off the coast of North Carolina in 1996.

Above: Early 19th-century painting of an English captain capturing a French privateer.

Blackbeard's pirate flag, or Jolly Roger, showed a horned skeleton holding an hourglass.

Bartholomew Roberts' flag. ABH stood for "A Barbadian's Head" and AMH for "A Martiniquan's Head" (both Caribbean islanders).

Stede Bonnet's flag had a dagger and heart flanking a skull and bone.

FAMOUS PIRATES

Sir John Hawkins (1532–95), Elizabethan commander; ship Jesus of Lubeck.

Sir Francis Drake (c. 1543–96), English hero (pirate to the Spanish!); ship Pelican (renamed Golden Hind).

Sir Christopher Myngs (1625–66), English buccaneer who commanded a pirate fleet off Jamaica; ship Marston Moor.

Jean-David Nau, "L'Olonnais" (c. 1635–67), French buccaneer known as the "Flail of the Spaniards."

Sir Henry Morgan (1635–88), Welsh buccaneer, sailed 36 ships and 2,000 men to destroy Panama City.

Edward Teach, "Blackbeard" (c. 1680–1718), famous English pirate; ship Queen Anne's Revenge.

Stede Bonnet (c. 1680–1718), English former plantation owner known as the "gentleman pirate," ship Revenge.

Bartholomew Roberts, "Black Barty" (c. 1682–1722), Welsh pirate killed by grapeshot from a British warship.

"Calico" Jack Rackham (c. 1690–1721), English pirate; ship Revenge, hanged in Jamaica.

Mary Read (c. 1695–1721), English pirate, died in a Jamaican prison.

Anne Bonny (c. 1697–1725), Irish pirate who sailed with Rackham.

The British, Dutch, and French in Latin America

In addition to Portugal, other European nations were not happy simply to allow Spain to dominate the Central and South American region. British and French privateers began carrying out raids on parts of the Spanish-controlled West Indies in the 16th century. Both countries then founded colonies on the small Lesser Antilles islands. They were followed by the Dutch, though the three nations tried to keep their colonies from trading with other countries. This and the wish for territory led to disagreements between all the major European powers.

This stamp was used with red ocher pigment to make tattoos by native people of the Caribbean islands before the arrival of the Europeans.

Dutch naturalists were amazed at the animals and plants they found in Brazil, including the anteater.

The Dutch in the Caribbean

The Dutch occupied a group of small islands off the Caribbean coast of the Spanish viceroyalty of Peru (modern Venezuela). In 1643 they settled Curaçao, which had been first visited by the Spanish more than 140 years earlier, and made it a trading island for the region. In the following century, Curaçao became the center of the Caribbean slave trade. It was later part of the Netherlands Antilles, which included Bonaire and Aruba.

The British

Beginning in the 1620s, the British claimed many islands of the Lesser Antilles. Early possessions included Saint Kitts, Barbados, Nevis, Antigua, Montserrat, and Jamaica. Later in the century, slaves were brought from Africa to work on sugar plantations, but the owners often returned to Britain once they had made their fortune. The British also founded settlements on the Caribbean coast of Belize, where they found and cut logwood trees to produce useful dyes.

The French

The French had tried to establish a settlement at Rio de Janeiro in the mid-16th century, but were driven out by the Portuguese. They were more successful further north, and they drove the Dutch out of what became French Guiana in 1667. By then the islands of Guadeloupe and Martinique had passed to the French crown. All three territories remain departments of France to this day. Toward the end of the 17th century the French gained the western part of Hispaniola and began taking African slaves there to work on coffee plantations.

An 18th-century painting of a West Indian Creole woman with her African servant.

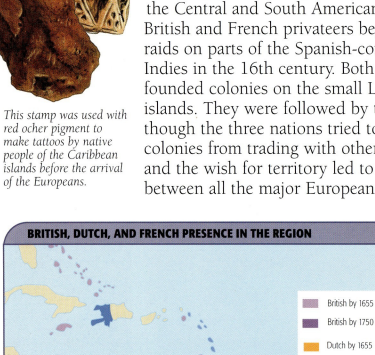

BRITISH, DUTCH, AND FRENCH PRESENCE IN THE REGION

British by 1655
British by 1750
Dutch by 1655
Dutch by 1750
French by 1655
French by 1750

Caribbean Sea

ATLANTIC OCEAN

SOUTH AMERICA

The Three Powers' Control and Settlement
The map shows the extent of British, Dutch, and French settlement throughout the region of coastal South America, the larger Caribbean islands of the Greater Antilles, and the much smaller islands of the Lesser Antilles. The total land areas settled were very small compared with the enormous Spanish colonies and Portuguese Brazil, but they gave the three other powers a colonial foothold in the region.

This 16th-century engraving of a native Brazilian celebration was made by a Flemish artist.

Battle for Brazil

The Dutch West India Company was formed to try and break the economic stranglehold held by Spain and Portugal in the Americas. The newly independent Dutch sent a Company fleet to Brazil in 1630, and they captured Pernambuco. A prince of the House of Orange was chosen to govern the small colony, and Dutch artists and scientists were invited to sample and describe the delights of South America. By the middle of the century, however, the Dutch had been driven out of Brazil.

Below: This 17th-century map shows the Dutch colony at Pernambuco.

THE BRITISH, DUTCH, AND FRENCH

1621
Dutch West India Company is founded.

1623–25
The British occupy Saint Kitts and then Barbados.

1635
First French colonies established in Guadeloupe and Martinique.

1638
Shipwrecked British sailors establish a settlement in Belize.

1654
The Portuguese drive the Dutch from Brazil.

1655
British forces capture Jamaica from the Spanish.

1667
French Guiana is awarded to France by the Treaty of Breda.

1697
The French take control of the western third of Hispaniola, named Saint Domingue (modern Haiti).

Trade and Industry

Transatlantic trade was based on produce from the Americas, manufactured goods from Europe, and slaves from Africa. The American produce began with brazilwood and sugar, to which were added tobacco and furs from the north. Along with imported slaves, Native Americans provided the labor in many colonial industries. In the fur trade (see page 27), Europeans found it useful to make alliances with native tribes. The colonists were constantly on the lookout for new opportunities, such as coffee, which was introduced to Brazil in the early 18th century.

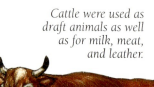

Cattle were used as draft animals as well as for milk, meat, and leather.

Brazilwood and Cattle

The attraction of brazilwood (also known as dyewood) to the colonists was that the core of this tropical hardwood gave a red pigment that was found to be ideal for dyeing cloth. This was very useful to the European textile industry, and the Portuguese colony was eventually named after its vital resource and first export. During the 1530s cattle were introduced to the colony to meet the demand for meat. As cattlemen needed more land for grazing, they moved to the interior of the region.

Leaves and flowers of the brazilwood tree.

Sugar Cane

Sugar cane was not native to the Americas, but it quickly became a most important resource. The Portuguese had experience of growing it on their Atlantic islands, and cane was first planted in Brazil around 1516. Soon large plantations were producing quantities of a substance that gradually replaced honey as a sweetener in European food. Around the middle of the 17th century the focus of sugar production and export shifted to the Caribbean islands.

Below: In the early days sugar cane was harvested by Native American workers. They were later replaced by slaves brought for the purpose from Africa.

1 The harvested cane stalks were taken to a mill, where they were crushed and produced a sugary juice.

2 The juice was treated with lime and then boiled in kettles over a brick furnace.

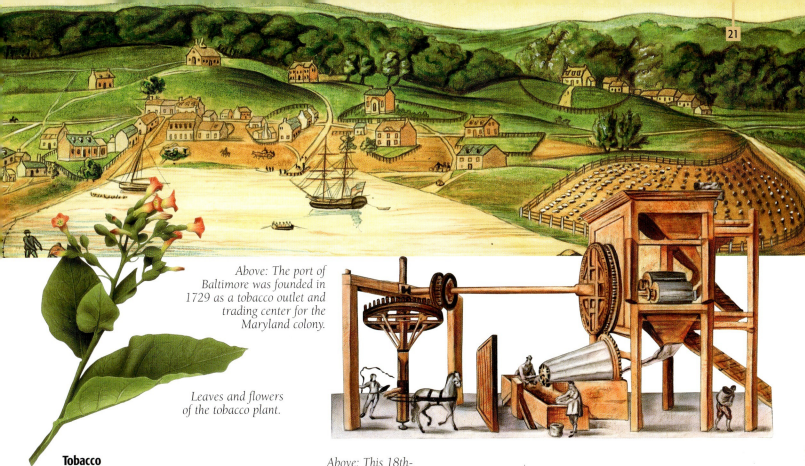

Above: The port of Baltimore was founded in 1729 as a tobacco outlet and trading center for the Maryland colony.

Leaves and flowers of the tobacco plant.

Tobacco

Native Americans had long been smoking dried leaves from the tobacco plant when the Europeans arrived. Colonists were cultivating tobacco in Hispaniola by 1531, in Brazil by 1600 (by which time it had been exported and introduced throughout Europe), and in Virginia by 1612. Demand for tobacco quickly grew in Europe, where it was exchanged for manufactured goods.

Above: This 18th-century engraving shows dried tobacco leaves being sieved by machine at the Royal Tobacco Factory in Mexico.

3   *The boiled juice was then skimmed with long-handled dippers as it crystallized and produced sugar.*

COLONIAL POWERS AND TRADE ROUTES

NORTH AMERICA

EUROPE

AFRICA

SOUTH AMERICA

PACIFIC OCEAN

ATLANTIC OCEAN

British	Portuguese	→ Meat, grains	→ Sugar
Dutch	Spanish	→ Manufactured goods	→ Fish
French		→ Spices, fabrics, tea, coffee	→ Slaves
			→ Rum

The Transatlantic Economy

The map shows the triangle of trade between Europe, Africa, and the Americas in the mid-18th century. Spain, Portugal, and the other colonial powers were driven by a firm belief that all trade generated wealth, which meant it had to be encouraged and protected to the full. They also believed that the colonies existed only to benefit the mother country, so exploitation was seen in a positive light.

The British in North America

The first British colony in North America, established on Roanoke Island in the 1580s, was doomed to fail. It was not until twenty years later that the British succeeded in establishing their first permanent colony. Life in this and successive settlements was hard, but the Puritan colonists were well suited to the difficulties. Many battles were fought and some treaties made with the Native Americans whose homelands the settlers invaded. By 1670 the British had established 12 of the original Thirteen Colonies (see pages 28–29), and the settlements were growing fast.

This Native American buckskin cloak is known as Powhatan's Mantle. It was named after the chief of the tribe that attacked Jamestown.

EARLY BRITISH SETTLEMENTS

PLYMOUTH
NEW YORK
PHILADELPHIA
JAMESTOWN
CHARLESTON

Area of British settlement

British Claims

King James I chartered the London Company and the Plymouth Company to form trading colonies in North America in 1606. The colonies belonged to the crown, which issued permits to investment companies, groups, and individuals. Colonies then offered cheap land to encourage settlers, and in some cases reserved some land for public use. This map shows the extent of British settlement about 100 years after the original charter.

Jamestown

The first permanent colony was formed by 104 men and boys, who arrived in America in three ships. They named their settlement Jamestown, after the English king. They were soon followed by more settlers, including women, but the first years of the colony were very hard. The land was swampy, safe drinking water was scarce, and the settlers faced starvation, disease, and attacks by native inhabitants. Nevertheless, by 1619 the colony's population numbered about a thousand.

Below: In January 1608 all the houses in Jamestown were destroyed by fire. The fortified settlement had to be completely rebuilt.

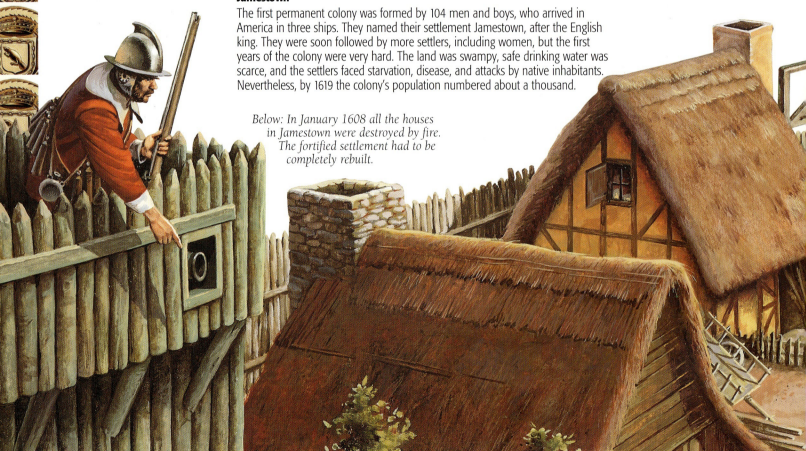

Thanksgiving

The Puritans who founded Plymouth colony in December 1620 had a harsh first winter in America. About half their number of 102 men, women, and children died. But by the following summer, despite poor crops of peas and wheat, the settlers' maize was growing well. In the early autumn of 1621, the governor of the colony called for a festival to thank God for the harvest. The Thanksgiving feast included goose, turkey, and fish, as well as fruit, vegetables, and cornbread. Some Native Americans also took part in the outdoor festival.

Craftworkers of the Delaware tribe wove wampum belts (made of shell beads) to commemorate their treaty with Penn.

Colonists soon came to appreciate native foods such as squash, corn, and beans.

Pennsylvania

In 1681 Charles II granted territory to the west of the Delaware River to William Penn (1644–1718). The grant was in settlement of a debt to Penn's father, who had been a distinguished admiral, and the region was named Pennsylvania in the admiral's honor. William Penn was a Quaker, and he saw the new colony as a refuge for those who shared his beliefs. In 1683 Penn signed a peace treaty and land-purchase agreement with local Native Americans. As governor, Penn introduced the colony's first constitution.

BRITISH SETTLEMENTS

1607
First permanent British settlement in America is established at Jamestown.

1614
Native American chief's daughter Pocahontas marries settler and tobacco-grower John Rolfe.

1620
The Puritan Pilgrim Fathers arrive in the Mayflower and found Plymouth settlement.

1624
King James I makes Virginia (including Jamestown) a royal colony.

1664
The British take control of the future Pennsylvania region from the Dutch.

1670
First permanent European settlement in South Carolina (near Charleston).

1676
Colonists rebel against the government in Virginia.

1691
Massachusetts (including Plymouth) and Maryland become royal colonies.

The Dutch and the Swedish in North America

S ettlements and ownership of land in the colony of New Netherland were encouraged and funded by the Dutch West India Company, which was granted a charter to develop trade with the Americas. For 17 years the Dutch were joined by Swedish and Finnish colonists sent by the rival New Sweden Company. Competition between the two colonies ended in Dutch victory, though the Swedes and other nationalities were allowed to stay and continue their own customs. In its turn, New Netherland eventually fell to the British.

Peter Stuyvesant lost a leg fighting for the Dutch in 1644. In this illustration he rebukes a cobbler who dared criticize his autocratic methods.

Peter Stuyvesant

Peter Stuyvesant (c.1592–1672) was director general of all the Dutch possessions in North America and the Caribbean. He was a tough, autocratic leader, disliked by many of the New Amsterdam colonists, who saw him as too devoted to the interests of the West India Company. Stuyvesant responded by establishing a municipal government for the city, which he still dominated. After being ousted by the British, Stuyvesant settled on his *bouwerij* (farm) in New York, after which the Bowery district is named.

The official seal of New Netherland.

The skyline of New Amsterdam included a windmill, Reformed church, weighing beam, and gallows.

The Dutch Buy Manhattan

In 1625, a group of Dutch colonists built a fort on Manhattan island and named their settlement New Amsterdam. A year later, the Dutch governor Peter Minuit bought the island from native Manates tribesmen for beads and trinkets worth 60 Dutch guilders. Over the next few years Breuckelen (now Brooklyn) and other settlements were established. In 1629, the Dutch brought in the patroon system by which any West India Company member who settled 50 colonists within four years became a land owner (patroon) who effectively controlled the settlers' lives.

NIEUW AMSTERDAM
op t Eylant Manhattans.

NEW AMSTERDAM

1621
Dutch West India Company is founded.

1624
Dutch West India Company establishes New Netherland at Fort Orange (now Albany, New York).

1638
First Swedish settlement is founded on the River Delaware.

1646
Peter Stuyvesant is appointed director general of New Netherland.

1655
The Dutch take over New Sweden.

1664
New Amsterdam falls to a British fleet and is renamed New York (after the Duke of York, later King James II).

1673–74
The Dutch briefly retake New York, before it becomes British again under the Treaty of Westminster.

British New York

The fierce trading rivalry between the British and the Dutch led to a fleet of British warships attacking New Netherland in 1664. Many of the Dutch colonists refused to fight for their despotic governor, and the British captured the colony. It came under the control of the Duke of York, for which he paid 40 beaver skins a year to his brother, King Charles II.

The Kalmar Nyckel was one of the two ships that sailed from Sweden in 1638. This sturdy ship made four return crossings of the Atlantic.

The Old Swedes Church, in present-day Wilmington, was built by Lutheran colonists in 1698.

New Sweden

The only Swedish colony in America was founded at Fort Christina (named after the Swedish queen), now Wilmington, Delaware. The first expedition was led by Dutchman Peter Minuit (see opposite) and included Swedish, Finnish, Dutch, and German settlers, who became farmers and fur traders. Unfortunately for the Scandinavians, the colony lay within the territory of New Netherland, and Peter Stuyvesant eventually forced them to surrender.

The French and Louisiana

In 1674, just eleven years after the establishment of New France as a royal province further north, French explorers were canoeing down the Mississippi River. This allowed them to expand their fur-trading activities further south. The provincial governor had hoped that this waterway would lead to the west and Asia, but by 1682 the explorers had reached the Gulf of Mexico and claimed the entire region drained by the river for France. This led to the establishment of the colony of Louisiana.

Portrait of Jean-Baptiste Le Moyne, Sieur de Bienville (1680–1768).

FRENCH SETTLEMENT

1674
Jolliet and Marquette explore the Mississippi basin.

1682
La Salle leads a canoeing expedition down the Mississippi River.

1688
La Salle's settlement at Fort St. Louis (near Victoria, Texas) is destroyed by Karankawa tribesmen.

1699
French Jesuits found a mission at the fur-trading post of Cahokia, Illinois; Le Moyne establishes the colony of Louisiana.

1701–12
Sieur de Bienville is governor of Louisiana.

1702
Fort Louis de la Mobile (near Mobile, Alabama) becomes capital of Louisiana colony.

1718
Sieur de Bienville founds the city of New Orleans.

Louisiana

In 1682 La Salle claimed the entire Mississippi valley for France, naming it Louisiana in honor of his king, Louis XIV. Seventeen years later, Pierre Le Moyne established the colony of Louisiana at Biloxi Bay (now Ocean Springs, Mississippi). Pierre and his brother Jean-Baptiste were sons of the French colonist and fur trader Charles Le Moyne. The brothers built forts near the mouth of the great river, which helped persuade their king to colonize the region.

Down the Mississippi

The French first explored the Mississippi when the governor of New France sent explorer Louis Jolliet and Jesuit missionary Jacques Marquette from Lake Michigan to see whether the great river flowed west to the Pacific. They reached the confluence of the Arkansas River. Eight years later, René-Robert Cavelier (Sieur de La Salle) canoed the entire length of the river and reached its mouth at the Gulf of Mexico.

This flint cross, made by native Illinois tribesmen, was given to Father Marquette.

THE FRENCH IN NORTH AMERICA

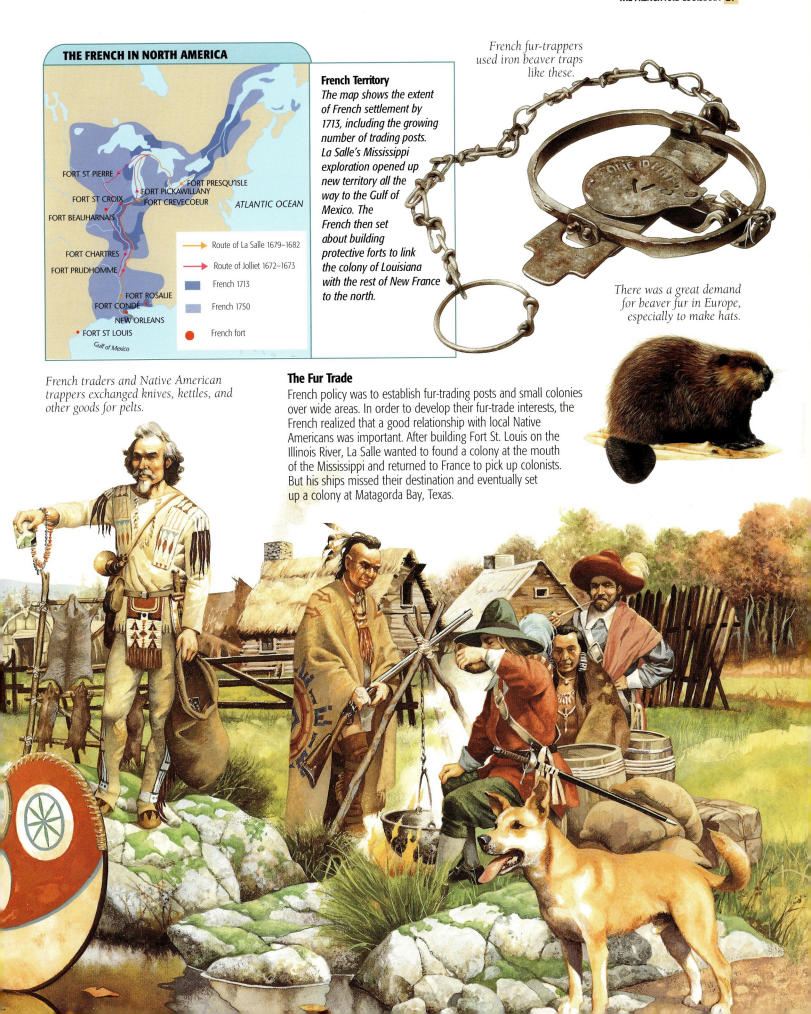

FORT ST PIERRE

FORT PRESQU'ISLE

FORT ST CROIX

FORT PICKAWILLANY

FORT CREVECOEUR

FORT BEAUHARNAIS

ATLANTIC OCEAN

FORT CHARTRES

FORT PRUDHOMME

→ Route of La Salle 1679–1682

→ Route of Jolliet 1672–1673

FORT ROSALIE

French 1713

FORT CONDÉ

French 1750

NEW ORLEANS

● FORT ST LOUIS

● French fort

Gulf of Mexico

French Territory

The map shows the extent of French settlement by 1713, including the growing number of trading posts. La Salle's Mississippi exploration opened up new territory all the way to the Gulf of Mexico. The French then set about building protective forts to link the colony of Louisiana with the rest of New France to the north.

French fur-trappers used iron beaver traps like these.

There was a great demand for beaver fur in Europe, especially to make hats.

French traders and Native American trappers exchanged knives, kettles, and other goods for pelts.

The Fur Trade

French policy was to establish fur-trading posts and small colonies over wide areas. In order to develop their fur-trade interests, the French realized that a good relationship with local Native Americans was important. After building Fort St. Louis on the Illinois River, La Salle wanted to found a colony at the mouth of the Mississippi and returned to France to pick up colonists. But his ships missed their destination and eventually set up a colony at Matagorda Bay, Texas.

The Thirteen Colonies

The Liberty Bell was ordered from England in 1751 to celebrate the 50th anniversary of Penn's Charter of Privileges. Today it hangs in a pavilion near Independence Hall in Philadelphia.

During the 17th century small American settlements grew into larger colonies. By the mid-1700s, they formed 13 British colonies that stretched down the coast from New England to Georgia (the last of the 13). Each colony had its own governor and laws, but all were subject to British control. French territorial claims ended in 1763, but by this time restrictive British trade laws and taxes were causing unrest among the colonists.

Title page of a book published in 1812.

Colonial Government

Powerful governors introduced different "frames of government" to their territories, some more liberal than others. In Pennsylvania, William Penn created a council that proposed laws and an assembly that approved them. Then, in 1701, he granted a new constitution, called the Charter of Privileges, which gave all lawmaking power to the lower house of the assembly. The charter was a great step forward towards liberal self-government.

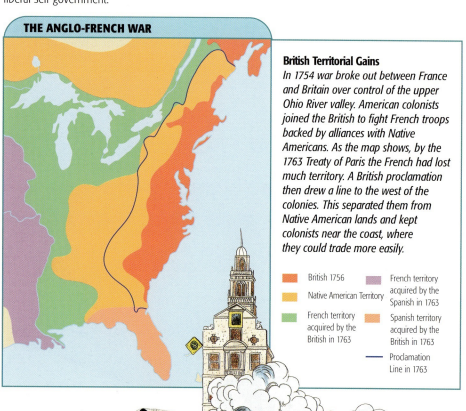

THE ANGLO-FRENCH WAR

British Territorial Gains

In 1754 war broke out between France and Britain over control of the upper Ohio River valley. American colonists joined the British to fight French troops backed by alliances with Native Americans. As the map shows, by the 1763 Treaty of Paris the French had lost much territory. A British proclamation then drew a line to the west of the colonies. This separated them from Native American lands and kept colonists near the coast, where they could trade more easily.

■ British 1756	■ French territory acquired by the Spanish in 1763
■ Native American Territory	
■ French territory acquired by the British in 1763	■ Spanish territory acquired by the British in 1763
	— Proclamation Line in 1763

This engraving of the Boston Massacre was made by the famous patriot Paul Revere.

The Boson Tea Party

On December 16, 1773, anti-British rebels disguised as Native Americans got onto British ships in Boston harbor. The rebels protested against taxes and the power of the British East India Company by throwing more than 300 chests of tea overboard. This act of defiance, which became known as the "Boston Tea Party," led to tough countermeasures that further united the colonists.

The Boston Massacre

On March 5, 1770, British troops reacted to street protests against new colonial taxes. Soldiers fired into an angry crowd outside the Customs House in Boston, killing three people and injuring others. American revolutionaries called the incident the "Boston Massacre" and used it to provoke further opposition to British colonial policies.

Right: This cartoon of 1774 shows protestors forcing tea down the throat of a tax collector.

Above: During the Boston Tea Party a group of about 60 American patriots attacked the tea chests of three ships in Boston harbor.

Navigation Acts

Beginning in 1651, Navigation Acts were passed by the English parliament to protect its trade and shipping. Some were aimed at the American colonies and the Dutch, to stop them profiting from trade between the West Indies and Europe. Goods such as sugar, cotton, and tobacco had to be shipped on English vessels, and from 1663 all European goods bound for the American colonies had to pass through an English port and were subject to duty.

Portrait of Thomas Hancock (1702–64), a wealthy Bostonian merchant who flouted regulations in shipping goods to and from the colonies.

THIRTEEN COLONIES

Virginia
(first permanent settlement 1607), began at Jamestown, became a royal colony in 1624.

Massachusetts
(settled 1620), started by Pilgrims at Plymouth, which became part of the larger colony in 1691.

New Hampshire
(settled 1623), ruled by the government of Massachusetts Bay, became a colony in 1679.

New York
(settled 1624), became a royal colony in 1685.

Connecticut
(settled 1633), became a colony in 1636.

Maryland
(settled 1634), founded by a family of wealthy Roman Catholics.

Rhode Island
(settled 1636), granted a charter in 1644, became a colony in 1647.

Delaware
(settled 1638), part of Pennsylvania until 1704, when it gained its own assembly.

Pennsylvania
(settled 1643), under liberal policies of William Penn became the most prosperous colony.

North Carolina
(settled 1653), constitution first drafted in 1669.

New Jersey
(settled 1660), first government in 1665, made a royal colony in 1702.

South Carolina
(settled 1670), separated from North Carolina in 1729.

Georgia
(settled 1733), founded by wealthy settlers as colony of small farms, became a royal colony in 1752.

Around the Hearth

The kitchen was the main room, where the whole family gathered to go about their daily business. All the cooking took place there, with pots hung or placed over the blazing fire. The fireplace had an opening in the brick or stone back wall for an oven. As well as cooking and eating in the kitchen, family members used its simple, solid furniture—chiefly made of oak—to sit and work, read, and talk.

A copper coffee pot and kettle. Metal was scarce, so utensils such as these were prized.

The frame of a colonial house built about 1698 in Massachusetts. It shows heavy planks held together by carved joints.

Houses

Most colonial homes in America were based on the style of late medieval English houses. The most important building material was wood, which was plentiful in the eastern forests of North America. Rectangular timber-frame houses were built around a large chimney, since winters could be very cold. The sloping roof was usually thatched or shingled, and the outside walls were finished with weatherproof clapboard. Interior walls were often made of plaster, and windows were generally small.

The Colonial Home

Early settlers in the American colonies built dwellings based on those they had inhabited in their home countries. But they were forced to adapt styles and building methods to local conditions, and this generally meant a dependence on wood. Though families were large, houses did not have many separate living rooms or bedrooms, so family members of all ages spent a great deal of time together. The style of living was simple, and this suited many settlers. Around 1700 the European colonists numbered about 300,000, and by 1775 this population had risen to 2.5 million.

Family Life

Families in the colonies generally had many children. Men normally married around the age of 21, and women around 18, but they usually stayed at one of their parents' homes. This was useful to everyone, because a large family made it easier to develop a farm or business. The father was head of the household, and he and his wife felt that their children provided security for their old age. Many households also included grandparents, aunts and uncles, and cousins. They all tried to help towards the success and well-being of the family.

Below: The kitchen served many purposes and was the hub of the colonial home.

This well-crafted walnut cradle from Delaware dates from about 1800.

Food

Learning from the difficulties of the earliest settlers, colonists came to appreciate native foods, such as cornbread, roasted squash, and acorn oil. Women also used maize to make hominy (from hulled corn) and succotash (with corn and beans). The main meal was eaten around midday, and it often consisted of a meat and vegetable stew. The most common meat was pork, and colonists kept sheep and chickens as well as pigs. Wild turkey and deer were sometimes added to the diet. A favorite drink was home-brewed beer sweetened with molasses or pumpkin.

Left: A pot for serving hot milk curdled with beer, and a storage jar for sack (strong white wine).

SACK 1646

TIMELINE

1774
The First Continental Congress meets in Philadelphia.

1775
April 19, first skirmishes at Lexington and Concord; May 10, the Second Continental Congress meets; June 17, the British drive the Americans from Breed's Hill in the Battle of Bunker Hill.

1776
July 4, the Declaration of Independence is adopted; September 15, the British occupy New York City.

1777
September 26, The British occupy Philadelphia.

1777–78
Washington quarters his troops at Valley Forge, Pennsylvania, where they spend a harsh winter but emerge with greater discipline.

1778
The United States and France sign an alliance, and France declares war on Britain.

1779
Spain declares war on Britain.

1780
The Netherlands joins the US side; May 12, Charleston falls after a British siege.

The American Revolution

American colonists' resentment at British authoritarian rule led to the Thirteen Colonies forming a Continental Congress in 1774. The following year, as anti-British feeling grew, the first hostile skirmishes took place between American militiamen and British troops. These battles marked the beginning of the American Revolution (1775–83), also known as the Revolutionary War in America or (in Britain) the War of American Independence. The French, Spanish, and Dutch took the opportunity to help reduce British control of America.

Commander in Chief

George Washington (1732–99) came from a wealthy Virginian family and fought for the British in the Anglo-French War. In 1775 Congress unanimously elected him commander in chief of the American forces, though he had not sought the position. He won ordinary American people over to the cause, and they saw him as a symbol of independence. Washington played a major role in the colonies' struggle for independence.

Detail of a painting showing Washington crossing the Delaware River in December, 1776. This led to an inspirational victory at Trenton, New Jersey.

A surveying compass owned by George Washington, who was a professional surveyor in civilian life.

Conflicting Armies

The American forces were first made up of militiamen, who fought for their separate colonies. They expected to fight for a short time and then return home. In 1775 Congress established the Continental Army, with an overall commander and a series of generals. They brought training and discipline to their troops, much needed to combat the British soldiers (known as "redcoats" because of their uniforms). The British army was a professional force, including foreign mercenaries hired from German princes.

Revolutionary Hero

Benjamin Franklin was born in Boston and at first wanted the American Colonies to stay in the British Empire. But he also wanted just rights for the colonists, and these were not granted. Franklin tried unsuccessfully to get French Canadians to join the war, and in 1776 was sent by Congress to France as a commissioner. There he was seen as a hero, leading his people to freedom from its feudal past.

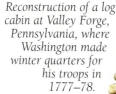

Reconstruction of a log cabin at Valley Forge, Pennsylvania, where Washington made winter quarters for his troops in 1777–78.

Portrait of Benjamin Franklin (1706–90), famous scientist, author, and diplomat.

Left: The original Declaration of Independence was written and signed on parchment.

The Declaration of Independence

In June 1776, Congress set up a committee to draft a declaration, and Thomas Jefferson of Virginia was appointed to complete this. Delegates debated the draft, which was formally adopted on July 4. The Declaration was printed and read out to a large crowd in Philadelphia days later. It famously stated: "We hold these truths to be self-evident, that all men are created equal, that they are endowed by their Creator with certain unalienable rights, that among these are life, liberty, and the pursuit of happiness."

Below: Thomas Jefferson and his committee present the Declaration to the president of Congress, John Hancock.

The young French nobleman, Marquis de Lafayette, arrived in America in 1777 to fight for the colonists.

Foreign Allies

When the Americans beat the British at Saratoga in 1777, France realized that Britain might be defeated and decided to join the war. French troops played a decisive part in land battles, and the French navy supported the Americans by holding the British off at sea. The Spanish and Dutch navies also helped by keeping British ships occupied in Europe.

Legend says that a Philadelphia seamstress named Betsy Ross sewed the first Stars and Stripes flag in 1776.

The United States

Even after they had established a Congress, declared independence and won the Revolutionary War, the 13 former colonies were still separate states. However, their representatives soon took steps to complete unification by agreeing a Constitution and setting up a federal government. Objections by individual states were overcome by allowing them to retain certain powers and making sure the new government represented all of them fairly, irrespective of their size. By 1789 the United States had their first president, George Washington.

Drawing of the Great Seal of the United States by Charles Thomson, Secretary of Congress. The seal was adopted in 1782.

New Government

In 1787 state delegates met in Philadelphia to discuss a new constitution. Agreement was finally reached, and by 1790 all thirteen states had ratified the new system. The federal government was to have three branches: an executive, headed by a president; a legislature, with two parts (a House of Representatives and a Senate); and a judiciary. The Constitution referred to citizens as "We the people of the United States."

James Madison of Virginia formulated many of the federal agreements and is often called the "Father of the Constitution". He became the fourth US president in 1809.

Women vote in New Jersey. This was the only state to give women this right (and only from 1790 to 1807).

THE UNITED STATES IN 1803

The Louisiana Purchase

In 1803 the Senate approved the wish of President Thomas Jefferson to accept an offer from Napoleon to buy the French territory of Louisiana (see page 26). The United States paid $15 million for a vast tract of land between the Mississippi River and the Rocky Mountains, stretching from the Gulf of Mexico to Canada. As the map shows, the new territory doubled the size of the new nation.

Gulf of Mexico

■ States by 1803	■ Northwest Territory	■ Other territory in present-day United States
■ Louisiana Purchase 1803	■ Other territories	

The British Surrender

George Washington and his American army were helped by French land and sea forces at Yorktown. A joint army besieged the British under General Lord Cornwallis at the tobacco port in Virginia. Any potential help from the British navy was stopped by a French fleet of 24 ships that closed off Chesapeake Bay. Cornwallis was left with no alternative but to surrender, and about 8,000 British troops were taken prisoner.

*Left: In this painting,
Siege of Yorktown,
French general Comte de
Rochambeau (pointing)
and George Washington
(to his left) discuss
strategy.*

Independent States

The original colonies made up the first 13 states, but they formed a loose confederation. Each state had its own constitution and retained the right to regulate trade and collect taxes. Despite the fact that the 1781 Articles of Confederation had created a "perpetual union" between the states, people at first considered themselves citizens of their state rather than of a unified nation.

*Robert R. Livingston was US minister to
France from 1801 to 1804. He helped
negotiate the Louisiana Purchase in Paris.*

*This
English cartoon of
1782 shows
Britannia
making it up
with her
daughter
America.*

Dear Mama say no more about it

Be a good Girl and give me a Buſs

George for Ever

The Treaty of Paris

Benjamin Franklin and others negotiated the final peace treaty between the British and Americans, which was signed in Paris in 1783. The treaty recognized the independence of the United States, with boundaries extending west to the Mississippi River, north to Canada, and south to Florida (which Britain lost to Spain). The treaty also granted the Americans fishing rights off the coast of Newfoundland.

THE UNITED STATES

1781
October 19, British forces surrender at Yorktown, Virginia.

1783
September 3, peace treaty is signed between the British and Americans in Paris; separate peace treaties are signed between Britain and France, and Britain and Spain.

1784
Peace treaty between Britain and the Netherlands.

1787
State delegates agree a Constitution.

1789
George Washington is elected 1st president.

1791
10 amendments (known as the Bill of Rights) are added to the Constitution.

1791–96
Three new states added —Vermont, Kentucky, and Tennessee.

1797
John Adams becomes 2nd president.

1800
Congress moves from Philadelphia to Washington (the new capital).

1801
Thomas Jefferson becomes 3rd president.

1803
The Louisiana Purchase; Ohio becomes 17th state.

The Church in Latin America

From early in the 16th century the king of Spain was authorized by the Pope to found Roman Catholic churches and appoint all religious officials in Spanish America. The main aim was to convert the local population. It is said that in 1531 two visions of the Virgin Mary appeared to a native convert to the north of Mexico City and commanded that a church be built there. Today, the original church has been replaced with a new basilica.

Above: Painted image of the Virgin of Guadalupe. In 1754 the Pope made the Virgin of Guadalupe patroness of New Spain.

Above: The Truro Synagogue, at Newport, Rhode Island, is the oldest standing synagogue in the United States.

Witch Hunt

In the 17th century there was great fear of witchcraft and possession by the devil. The most famous witch hunt took place in Salem, Massachusetts, in 1692. When a group of teenage girls began having strange fits, parents and grandparents were arrested on suspicion of witchcraft. Nineteen men and women were convicted and hanged, and another male "witch" was pressed to death with stones. Many more were imprisoned, but released the following year.

The Inquisition

From the earliest times of European settlement, the Roman Catholic clergy held great power in the Spanish colonies. They saw it as their duty to convert Native Americans to Christianity. In 1569 King Philip II of Spain strengthened Catholic control by establishing tribunals of the Inquisition in both New Spain and Peru. Their main purpose was to seek out and punish heretics, who were burned at the stake if they refused to repent.

Native Americans were seen as savages by early Spanish conquerors. This victim was blessed by a clergyman as he was burned at the stake.

Religion in the New World

Religion played an important role in the colonization of the Americas. Roman Catholicism dominated Latin America, which did not escape the harsh attentions of the Inquisition. In the North American colonies, Protestants outnumbered other groups, though there were also Catholics and Jews. Many colonists had left Europe to escape persecution, and religious freedom was made law in the Bill of Rights of 1791. In the new United States, no religious group received official recognition as a state church.

Jewish Settlements

Many early American colonists were Jewish or *conversos* (Jews who had converted to Christianity). Some found their way illegally to the New World, since even "New Christians" were officially not allowed to emigrate. Many converted Portuguese merchants went to Brazil, and inquisitors in the colonies referred to all Jewish people as "Portuguese Jews." The Dutch offered more religious freedom, and the first Jewish community in North America was in New Amsterdam.

Right: In 1660, Mary Dyer was hanged for spreading Quaker beliefs in the colony of Massachusetts.

Toward Toleration

Religious tolerance was certainly not practised in all the American colonies. Puritans in New England wanted fellow colonists to worship in the same way, and those who failed to conform were sometimes fined, beaten, or imprisoned. The situation changed as groups with different religious views arrived. In New York and New Jersey there was no established church. In Pennsylvania and Delaware, all churches had freedom of worship. In 1649, Maryland's leaders passed a religious toleration act.

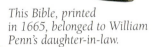

This Bible, printed in 1665, belonged to William Penn's daughter-in-law.

Below: This 19th-century painting shows the chaotic scene at the Salem witch trials.

Colonial Art and Architecture

The art and architecture of the American colonies naturally developed from European methods and styles. In Spanish and Portuguese South America, the Baroque style was most evident in architecture and sculpture. In North America, a naive form of painting was gradually replaced by more formal, refined techniques. Similar developments were seen in architecture, as colonists tried to match the sophistication of their mother country.

Left: A painted and gilded wooden image of the Virgin of Quito. It was made around 1750 in New Granada (modern Ecuador), from a model by Bernardo Legarda.

North American painters

Early colonial painters had no formal training. They created the simple, bold compositions that made up the folk art of the 17th century. Known as limners, folk artists earned a living by traveling around painting faithful, natural portraits of local residents. By the following century, American portrait painters were more influenced by the sophisticated styles of European art. Many had studied in Europe.

A limner's portrait of 1664.

Below: Portrait of silversmith and patriot Paul Revere painted in 1770 by John Singleton Copley of Boston.

Latin American artists

From the late 16th century, colonial painters, sculptors, and craftworkers belonged to European-style guilds. Indigenous artists learned European methods from engravings and prints. Many guilds did not allow non-Spaniards to reach the highest ranks, but some artists (such as the mestizo painter and sculptor Bernardo Legarda), produced brilliant work. Artists were dependent on commissions from patrons, and especially from the Roman Catholic Church.

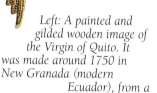

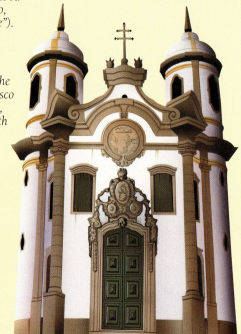

Left: The Church of São Francisco de Assis in Ouro Preto, Brazil, was designed in 1766 by Antonio Francisco Lisboa (known as Aleijadinho, meaning "little cripple").

Right: The façade of the Church of San Francisco Acatepec near Puebla, Mexico, is covered with glazed tiles. The church was built around 1760.

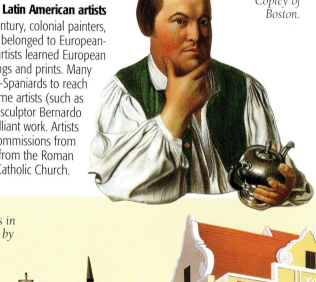

Spanish-American Architecture

Colonial architects followed Spanish styles, which native craftsmen learned to put into effect. The earliest public buildings were in the decorative Plateresque (or "silverwork") style. During the 17th century Baroque ornamentation became dominant, since this was the style supported by the Catholic Church and Spanish monarchy. The elaborate late-Baroque style known as Churrigueresque (after the Churriguera family of architects) was also evident in Spanish America.

Above: The Penha Building in Willemstad, Curaçao, was built in the Dutch style in 1708. The Netherlands took control of this Caribbean island in 1634.

The Peale Family painted about 1770 by Charles Willson Peale of Maryland. The artist's sons (named Raphaelle, Rembrandt, Rubens, and Titian) also became painters.

The Caribbean

The colonial powers of Spain, Britain, France, and the Netherlands took their own architectural styles and building methods to the islands of the West Indies. Public buildings were a way of showing national identity, which made colonial architecture all the more important.

Above: Destrehan Plantation, on the banks of the Mississippi in Louisiana, was built as a planter's family home in 1787. It shows the French Creole colonial style.

North America

Colonial architecture reflected European styles and varied according to national influences on individual colonies and, later, states. In the southern colonies, wealthy planters built large, comfortable homes. During the 18th century, the British colonies adopted a Georgian style that was formal, elegant, and well proportioned. Some early Georgian houses were built in Williamsburg, Virginia.

Left: Thomas Jefferson (who was US president from 1801 to 1809) designed this house, called Monticello, in the Neoclassical style. It was built near Charlottesville, Virginia, between 1769 and 1808, and it became the Jefferson family home.

TIMELINE

1604
Pierre du Gua (Sieur de Monts) and Samuel de Champlain found a settlement on an island in the St. Croix River.

1608
Founding of Quebec.

1610
Henry Hudson sails into what would become known as Hudson Bay.

1642
French missionaries found Montreal (originally called Ville-Marie).

1648–49
The Iroquois inflict heavy defeats on rival Hurons.

1654–70
Acadia comes under British rule.

1663
Company of New France is disbanded and the colony becomes a royal province.

1670
Hudson's Bay Company is founded by English merchants in London and granted a charter by King Charles II.

1672
Comte de Frontenac becomes governor general of New France.

1689–97
King William's War, British and Iroquois versus the French; overall, no major territorial gains are made.

Hudson's Bay Company

The company had sole trading rights in the region that formed the drainage basin of the Hudson Bay, where they soon built trading posts. The region was named Rupert's Land, after Prince Rupert, the company's first governor. Company agents got furs from Native American hunters, offering guns, knives, and kettles in exchange. They beat off competition from others to remain the biggest, most powerful fur-trading company.

A Hudson's Bay Company brass trading token. Furs were sold for tokens, which could be exchanged for European goods.

Early Canadian Settlements

French explorers established the first permanent settlements in what was to become Canada in the early 17th century. They founded the colony of New France and attracted many fur-trappers and traders to the region. Migration from Europe was slow, however. Conditions were harsh, relations with local Native American tribes were difficult, and the British were also keen to exploit the fur trade. This rivalry led to war between French and British colonists before the end of the century.

New France

The first permanent European settlement was founded in 1605 by Sieur de Monts and Champlain at Port Royal (near present-day Annapolis Royal, Nova Scotia). The region around the settlement became known as Acadia. Three years later, the two Frenchmen built a fur-trading fort on the St. Lawrence River at a place called Quebec, where they befriended the local Algonquin people. The wider region controlled by the French was soon called New France, and a company was set up to settle the colony.

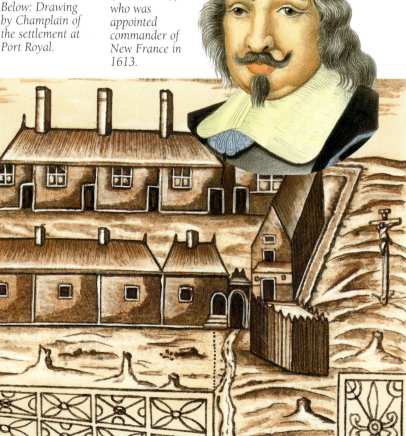

Below: Drawing by Champlain of the settlement at Port Royal.

Right: Samuel de Champlain (1567–1635), who was appointed commander of New France in 1613.

The King's Daughters

Before New France became a royal province, colonization was not successful. Almost all French settlers were men, and few took their wives and families. King Louis XIV decided to put this right by giving free passage and small dowries to healthy women of childbearing age. Known as the *Filles du Roi* (King's Daughters), more than 800 young women arrived in the colony between 1663 and 1673. Most found husbands, and the policy resulted in the population growing to about 8,500 by 1676.

The Iroquois

The fur trade in much of the New France region was controlled by a confederacy of Iroquois tribes whose lands covered the routes west. The French made enemies of the Iroquois by siding with rival tribes, which led to native warriors making many attacks on French settlements. In the late 1660s some Iroquois tribes were forced to make peace with the French.

This notched staff lists the five tribal groups of the Iroquois Great Council.

Anglo-French Rivalry

The success of the Hudson's Bay Company meant that New France was caught between the British in northern Rupert's Land and the Iroquois–who were supported by the British and Dutch–in the south. The French also wanted to dominate the fur trade, while many British colonists were pushing for more land for farming. In 1689 hostilities broke out at the start of the so-called King William's War, during which the British captured Fort Royal but failed to take Quebec.

Above: William of Orange, who ruled Britain as William III (1689–1702) together with his wife Mary II. He opposed France in Europe and North America.

Below: Some of the "King's Daughters" arriving in Quebec in 1667. They were presented first to Bishop François Laballe and Jean-Baptiste Talon, respectively bishop and royal agent of New France.

The Fight for Canada

There were two more Anglo-British wars in the first half of the 18th century, during which there were many skirmishes and some major battles, as the nations continued to dispute Canadian territory. Both wars involved the Native Americans whose original lands were being disputed by European settlers, and both sides were happy to seek the help of native allies. But the conflicts between the two nations were also linked to the wider issues fought over in the Wars of the Spanish and Austrian Succession.

WAR IN CANADA

1702–13
Queen Anne's War.

1710
The British capture Port Royal and Acadia from the French.

1711
Unsuccessful British and Iroquois attack on Quebec and Montreal.

1713
Treaty of Utrecht confirms loss of French territory.

1744–48
King George's War.

1748
Treaty of Aix-la-Chapelle gives captured territory back to Britain and France.

1749
A British naval base is established at Halifax, Nova Scotia.

1755
Beginning of deportation and exile of Acadians.

During Queen Anne's War, the British made an unsuccessful naval attack on Quebec.

Queen Anne's War

This war, named after Britain's Queen Anne (ruled 1702–14), broke out when French forces and their Algonquian allies raided British settlements. The British then made several attacks on Port Royal in Acadia, which they finally captured in 1710. The war ended with the signing of the Treaty of Utrecht, by which the French had to give up Nova Scotia, Newfoundland, and territory around Hudson Bay. But the treaty did not define the boundaries between the two nations' colonies clearly, so peace was not secured.

Portrait of Sir William Johnson, who encouraged and organized Iroquois war parties against the French.

ANGLO-FRENCH WARS

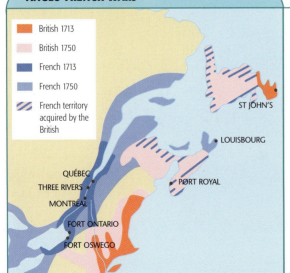

- British 1713
- British 1750
- French 1713
- French 1750
- French territory acquired by the British

ST JOHN'S
LOUISBOURG
QUÉBEC
THREE RIVERS
MONTRÉAL
PORT ROYAL
FORT ONTARIO
FORT OSWEGO

Territorial Changes

Territory was taken and retaken by both sides in the series of wars, and the periods between the wars were never entirely peaceful. The 1713 peace treaty gave important coastal territory to Britain, as shown on this map. By 1750 large stretches of territory had been acquired by both colonial nations, but New France had been squeezed into a narrow strip.

King George's War

The third Anglo-French colonial conflict was named after King George II, who ruled Britain from 1727 to 1760. It began when French forces tried and failed to retake Nova Scotia. The biggest victory went to the British in 1745, when naval ships and New England troops captured the important French fortress of Louisbourg on Cape Breton Island.

The city of Quebec.

Expulsion of the Acadians

In 1755, the British tried to force the French Acadians to swear an oath of allegiance to King George II. When the Acadians refused, the British decided to expel them. Some escaped to Quebec, but over the next few years many thousands were transported by ship to British colonies further south. Some made their way to French-ruled Louisiana, while others were eventually able to return to Nova Scotia and New Brunswick.

Left: Scalps were sometimes stretched on a wooden hoop, as in this 18th-century example.

Native Raids

Warfare was brutal among the British, French, and Native Americans. Many European settlers were killed by roaming bands of Native Americans. Some native warriors scalped dead victims to gain war trophies or even to exchange for the bounty that was offered as an incentive by the Europeans. Other settlers were taken prisoner, and some white captives adapted to tribal life and made little attempt to return to their colony.

An Algonquian war club.

Right: The Acadians were rounded up, ready to be put on board ship and transported south.

Under British Rule

The fourth and final Anglo-French War broke out over control of the upper Ohio River valley (see page 28). It led to the famous capture of Quebec by General Wolfe's British troops, and finally resulted in the surrender of New France to Britain in 1763. Twenty-eight years later, Britain divided the former colony of Quebec into the provinces of Upper and Lower Canada (the name coming from Iroquoian *kanata*, meaning "village"). By that time the British had lost control of their Thirteen American Colonies, adding importance to their Canadian possessions.

Chief Pontiac rallies his allied warriors to fight the British.

The Death of General Wolfe was painted about 1771 by the famous American artist Benjamin West.

After the Treaty of Paris

With the decline of French power, Native American tribes were concerned at the loss of their lands to British troops and colonists. Chief Pontiac of the Ottawa tribe, whose homelands were to the north of Lake Huron, set about uniting neighboring tribes to try to oust the invaders. Pontiac's warriors took many British fortified posts, but after some of his allies deserted him, the native leader was forced to make peace in 1766.

This print of the Battle of the Plains of Abraham shows all the action in one scene.

The Fall of New France to the British

In 1759 General James Wolfe led a British attack on Quebec, which was held by French troops under the Marquis de Montcalm. At first Wolfe's attacks failed, but then he audaciously ordered 5,000 troops to scale a steep cliff to the Plains of Abraham, near Quebec. The plan worked, but Wolfe was killed in the attack. The French general also died a few hours later. The loss of Quebec was decisive in the fall of New France to the British.

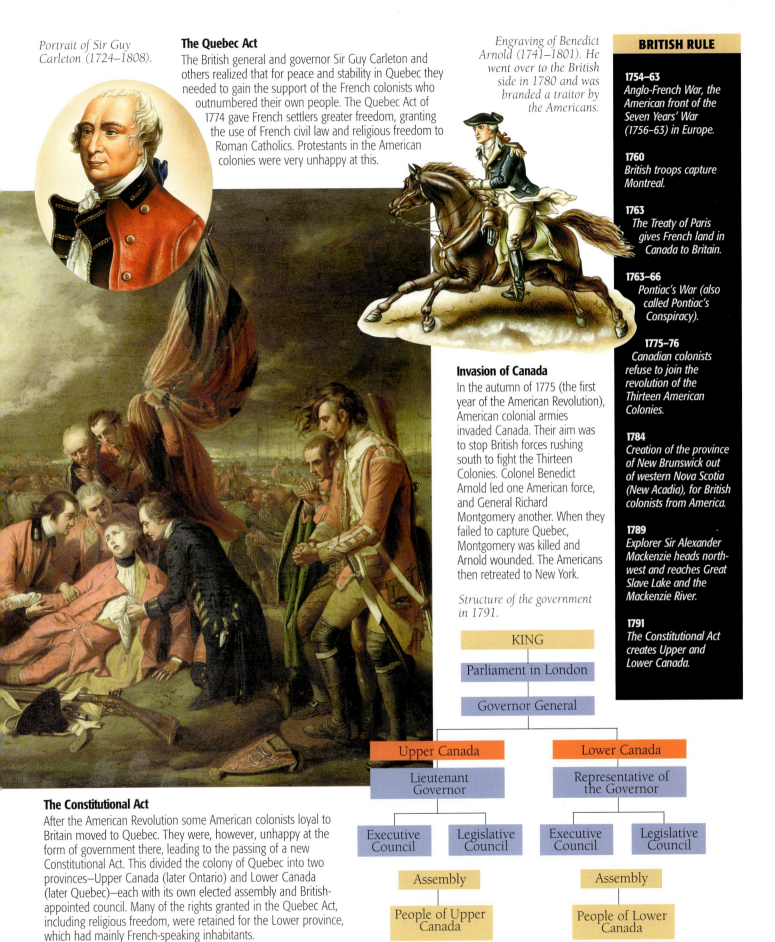

Portrait of Sir Guy Carleton (1724–1808).

The Quebec Act

The British general and governor Sir Guy Carleton and others realized that for peace and stability in Quebec they needed to gain the support of the French colonists who outnumbered their own people. The Quebec Act of 1774 gave French settlers greater freedom, granting the use of French civil law and religious freedom to Roman Catholics. Protestants in the American colonies were very unhappy at this.

Engraving of Benedict Arnold (1741–1801). He went over to the British side in 1780 and was branded a traitor by the Americans.

Invasion of Canada

In the autumn of 1775 (the first year of the American Revolution), American colonial armies invaded Canada. Their aim was to stop British forces rushing south to fight the Thirteen Colonies. Colonel Benedict Arnold led one American force, and General Richard Montgomery another. When they failed to capture Quebec, Montgomery was killed and Arnold wounded. The Americans then retreated to New York.

Structure of the government in 1791.

The Constitutional Act

After the American Revolution some American colonists loyal to Britain moved to Quebec. They were, however, unhappy at the form of government there, leading to the passing of a new Constitutional Act. This divided the colony of Quebec into two provinces—Upper Canada (later Ontario) and Lower Canada (later Quebec)—each with its own elected assembly and British-appointed council. Many of the rights granted in the Quebec Act, including religious freedom, were retained for the Lower province, which had mainly French-speaking inhabitants.

BRITISH RULE

1754–63
Anglo-French War, the American front of the Seven Years' War (1756–63) in Europe.

1760
British troops capture Montreal.

1763
The Treaty of Paris gives French land in Canada to Britain.

1763–66
Pontiac's War (also called Pontiac's Conspiracy).

1775–76
Canadian colonists refuse to join the revolution of the Thirteen American Colonies.

1784
Creation of the province of New Brunswick out of western Nova Scotia (New Acadia), for British colonists from America.

1789
Explorer Sir Alexander Mackenzie heads north-west and reaches Great Slave Lake and the Mackenzie River.

1791
The Constitutional Act creates Upper and Lower Canada.

KING

Parliament in London

Governor General

Upper Canada — Lower Canada

Lieutenant Governor — Representative of the Governor

Executive Council — Legislative Council — Executive Council — Legislative Council

Assembly — Assembly

People of Upper Canada — People of Lower Canada

Glossary

Archipelago An expanse of sea scattered with small islands.

Brazilwood Also known as dyewood, this tropical hardwood grew in Brazil (hence the name). It produced a valuable red dye that was used for dying cloth.

Buccaneer A pirate, especially one preying on Spanish settlements in the West Indies during the 17th century.

Bullion A precious metal, such as gold or silver, in bulk form.

Caravel A small Spanish or Portuguese ship of the 15th and 16th centuries. It had a broad bow and triangular sails.

Cargo The goods carried by a ship.

Cobbler A person who makes or repairs shoes.

Colony A group of settlers living in a new territory, which may already be occupied by indigenous (or native) people.

Colonization The process by which settlers—in this volume, European settlers—not only settled but completely took over the lands of the first indigenous inhabitants.

Creole A term invented in the 16th century that was originally used to describe people born in European colonies in the Americas and other parts of the world. Later came to refer to the languages spoken by these people, which were often a mix of European, African, and local languages.

Decentralise To move decision-making and / or government from large, central groups to smaller, local groups.

Doubloon A gold coin used in Spain and Spanish America.

Fluyt A Dutch cargo ship from the 17th century.

Galleon A heavy, square-rigged ship used between the 15th and 18th centuries. It was a vessel for war or trading.

Gallows A frame, usually made of wood, used to hang people.

Hominy A food dish made of dried maize (corn) kernels that have been treated with an alkali of some type. First made by Native Americans in present-day Guatemala at least 1500 years ago.

Hull The main body of a ship.

Indigenous Something that lives naturally in a particular region of the world.

Jesuits The Society of Jesus, whose members are known as Jesuits. Founded by Ignatius de Loyola in 1540. They opposed the Protestant Reformation and wanted to reform the Catholic Church from within. There were many Jesuit missions in the Americas.

Latitude The distance of a point from the equator, measured in a North–South direction.

Longitude The distance of a point from the equator, measured in a East–West direction.

Maize A tall cereal originally from Central America.

Missionary Someone who campaigns to increase membership of the Christian church, often through converting people from other religions.

Native American A person whose ancestors lived in the Americas before the European conquerors and settlers arrived.

Pilgrim A person who makes a journey to a sacred place to show their devotion to God.

Pilgrim Fathers (or Mothers) The early Puritan settlers at Plymouth colony in present-day Massachusetts.

Pirate A robber operating at sea.

Plantation A large farm or estate where valuable agricultural products such as cotton, tobacco, or sugar are cultivated, usually by slaves or resident laborers.

Privateer A privately owned ship that can be commissioned by a government to fight against the enemy in wartime. Also the name for the captain or crew of this kind of ship.

Puritans Protestants in 16th and 17th century England who wanted greater "purity" or reform of the church than what was carried out under the Reformation. Many Puritans migrated from England to North America where they set up colonies. The first and most well-known Puritans in America journied on the *Mayflower* and set up a colony at Plymouth in 1620.

Quakers The Religious Society of Friends, commonly known as the Quakers, was established in England in the 17th century by people who were unhappy with existing Christian churches. The Quakers were persecuted in England and many migrated to the North America in search of religious freedom.

Rigging The ropes used for controlling sails and supporting the mast on board a ship.

Rudder A flat piece attached to the base of a ship, at the stern. It allows it to change course.

Seaboard A coast, especially the Atlantic Seaboard, or eastern coast of North America.

Slave A person who is treated as the property of another and who is forced to work.

Stern The rear end of a ship.

Textile Fabric or cloth, usually made by weaving, knitting, or knotting fibers such as cotton or silk together.

Transatlantic trade Trade across the Atlantic Ocean, usually between Europe, Africa and the Americas.

Viceroy A governor of a province or colony who rules in place of a king or queen.

Viceroyalty The territory over which a viceroy rules.

Index

Acadia / Acadians 5, 40, 42, 43
Acapulco 4, 8
Adams, John 35
Africa 18, 20, 21
Aguirre, Ginés Andrés de 13
Albany 25
Aleijadinho 5
Algonquin people 40
Almagro, Diego de 10
Amazon River 15
American Revolution 32, 45
Andes Mountains 11
Anglo-French War 28, 32, 44, 45
Annapolis Royal 40
Antigua 18
Argentina 11
Arkansas River 26
Arnold, Benedict 45
Aruba 18
Asia 26
Austrian 42
Aztecs 6

Bahamas 16
Baja California 9
Baltimore 21
Barbados 18, 19
Battle of Bunker Hill 32
Battle of the Plains of Abraham 44
Belize 19
Biloxi Bay 26
Black Barty 17
Blackbeard 16, 17
Bolivia 10, 11
Bonaire 18
Bonnet, Stede 17
Bonny, Anne 16, 17
Boston 29
Boston Massacre 28, 29
Boston Tea Party 5, 28
Bourbon dynasty 5, 13
Brazil 5, 13, 14, 15, 18, 19, 20, 21, 37
Breed's Hill 32
Britain / British 5, 13, 16, 18, 22, 28, 32, 33, 35, 39, 40, 41, 42, 43, 44, 45
British East India Company 28
British Empire 32
Brooklyn 24
Buade, Louis de, Comte de Frontenac et de Palluau, Comte de 40
Buenos Aires 13

Cahokia, Illinois 26
Callao 10, 11

Canada / Canadians 4, 5, 6, 34, 35, 40, 42, 44
Canada, Lower 5, 44, 45
Canada, Upper 5, 44, 45
Cape Breton Island 42
Cape Cod 7
Captaincy System 14
Caribbean 4, 13, 17, 18, 20, 24, 38, 39
Caribbean Sea 16
Carleton, Sir Guy 45
Carolina 17
Cartagena 13, 16
Carvalho e Melo, Sebastião José de, Marques de Pombal 15
Cavelier, Renè-Robert (Sieur de La Salle) 26
Central America 4, 5, 6, 16, 18
Champlain, Samuel de 4, 40
Charcas 11
Charcas people 10
Charles II, of England, King 23, 40
Charles III, of Spain, King 12
Charleston 23, 32
Charlottesville 39
Charter of Privileges 28
Chesapeake Bay 35
Chile 11
Chinese 8
Cole, Humphrey 16
Colombia 13
Columbus, Christopher 5
Company of New France 40
Concord 32
Congonhas 5
Connecticut 29
Cornwallis, Charles, general 35
Council of the Indies 4, 9
Creole 13, 18, 39
Curacao 18
Cuzco 10

Declaration of Independence 32, 33
Delaware 23, 25, 29, 31, 37
Delaware River 23, 25, 32
Drake, Sir Francis 10, 16, 17
du Motier, Marie-Joseph Paul Yves Roch Gilbert, Marquis de Lafayette 33
Duke of York 25
Dutch 5, 13, 16, 17, 18, 19, 23, 24, 25, 32, 37, 41
Dutch West India Company 4, 19, 24, 25
Dyer, Mary 37

Ecuador 38
Elizabeth I, of England, Queen 17
England / English 4, 6, 13, 17
Europe 6, 13, 20, 21, 27, 38, 45

Far East 4
Finnish 24, 25
First Continental Congress 5, 32
Florida 13, 35
France / French 5, 6, 13, 18, 19, 26, 28, 32, 33, 35, 39, 41, 43
Francisco de Toledo 10
Francoise Laballe 41
Franklin, Benjamin 32, 35
French and Indian War 32, 45
French Canadians 32
French Guiana 18, 19

George II, of England, King 42, 43
George III, of England, King 6
Georgia 5, 28, 29
Germans 25
Great Slave Lake 45
Greater Antilles 18
Gua, Pierre du 4, 40
Guadeloupe 18, 19
Gulf of Mexico 8, 26, 27, 34

Habsburgs 13
Haiti 19
Halifax 42
Hancock, John 33
Hancock, Thomas 29
Havana 13
Hawkins, Sir John 17
Hispaniola 4, 8, 16, 19, 21
Hudson Bay 40
Hudson, Henry 40
Hudson's Bay Company 40, 41
Hurons 40

Illinois 26
Illinois River 27
Inca 6, 10, 13
Iroquois 40, 41, 42

Jamaica 16, 18, 19
James I, of England, king 22, 23
James II, of England, king 25
Jamestown 4, 22, 23, 29
Jefferson, Thomas 33, 34, 35, 39
Jesuits 13, 14, 15, 26
Joào III, of Portugal, king 14
Johnson, Sir William 42
Jolliet, Louis 26
Jolly Roger 17

Karankawa 26
Kentucky 35
King George's War 42
King William's War 5, 40, 41

L'Olonnais 17
La Plata (modern Sucre) 10, 11, 26
Lake Huron 44
Lake Michigan 26
Lake Texcoco 4
Latin America 6, 18, 36
Lely, Sir Peter 16
Le Moyne, Pierre 26
Le Moyne, Charles 26
Le Moyne, Jean-Baptiste 26
Legarda, Bernardo 38
Lesser Antilles 18
Lexington 32
Liberty Bell 28
Lima 10, 11
Lisboa, Antonio Francisco 38
Livingston, Robert R. 35
London Company 22
Louis XIV, of France, King 26, 41
Louisbourg 42
Louisiana 5, 26, 27, 39, 43
Louisiana Purchase 34, 35

Mackenzie River 45
Mackenzie, Alexander 45
Madison, James 34
Madrid 13
Manates 24
Manco Capuc 6, 10
Manhattan 24
Mariana Islands 8
Marquette, Jacques 26
Martim Afonso de Sousa 14
Martinique 18, 19
Maryland 5, 21, 23, 29, 37
Massachusetts 5, 23, 29, 30
Massachusetts Bay 29
Matagorda Bay 27
Mayflower 7, 23
Mendoza, Antonio de 8
Mexico 8, 9, 21
Mexico City 12, 13, 36
Miguel Cabrera 13
Minas Gerais 5, 15
Minuit, Peter 24
Mississippi 26, 27, 39
Mississippi River 26, 34, 35
Montcalm-Gozon, Louis-Joseph de, Marquis de Montcalm 44
Montgomery, Richard, General 45
Monticello 39

Montreal 5, 40, 42, 45
Montserrat 18
Morgan, Sir Henry 17
Myngs, Sir Christopher, 16, 17

Napoleon I, of France, Emperor 34
Nau, Jean-David, 17
Netherlands 6, 32, 35, 38, 39
Netherlands Antilles 18
Nevis 18
New Amsterdam 5, 24, 25, 37
New Brunswick 5, 43, 45
New England 28, 37, 42
New France 26, 27, 40, 42, 44
New Granada 38
New Hampshire 29
New Jersey 29, 34, 37
New Netherland 4, 24, 25
New Orleans 26
New Spain 8, 11, 13, 36
New Sweden 5, 25
New Sweden Company 24
New York 24, 25, 29, 32, 37
Newfoundland 35
North America 4, 17, 22, 24, 30, 37, 38
North Carolina 17, 29
Nova Scotia 40, 42, 43, 45

Ocean Springs 26
Ohio 35
Ohio River 28
Ohio River Valley 44
Ottawa tribe 44
Ouro Preto 38
Panama 11
Paraguay 11, 15
Peale, Charles Willson 39
Penn, William 23, 28,29, 37
Pennsylvania 7, 23, 28, 29
Pernambuco 19

Peru 6, 8, 11
Philadelphia 5, 28, 32, 33, 34, 35
Philip II, of Spain, king 36
Philippines 4, 8, 9
Pilgrims 4, 6, 7, 23, 29
Piracy 16
Pizarro, Francisco 4, 10, 11
Pizarro, Gonzalo 10
Plate River 15
Plymouth 4, 6, 23, 29
Plymouth Company 22
Pocahontas 4, 23
Pontiac, Chief 44
Pontiac's War 45
Port Royal 5, 40, 42
Portugal / Portuguese 5, 6, 13, 14, 15, 18, 19, 20, 21, 38
Potosí 11
Powhatan 22
Puebla 38
Puritans 22, 23

Quaker 7, 23
Quebec 4, 40, 41, 42, 43, 44, 45
Queen Anne's War 5, 42

Rackham, Calico Jack 16, 17
Read, Mary 16, 17
Revere, Paul 28, 38
Revolutionary War 34
Rhode Island 29
Rio de Janeiro 5, 15
Rio Rimac 11
Roanoke 22
Roberts, Bartholomew 17
Rochambeau, Comte de 35
Rocky Mountains 34
Rolfe, John 23
Ross, Betsy 33
Rubens 39
Rupert's Land 41

Saint Domingue 19
Saint Kitts 18, 19
Salem 36, 37
San José de Cabo 9
Santo Domingo 4, 8
Sào Paulo 5, 14, 15,
Saratoga 33
Second Continental Congress 32
Siege of Yorktown 35
Sieur de Bienville 26
Sieur de Monts, 40
South America 4, 5, 6, 10, 11, 16, 18, 19, 38
South Carolina 5, 23, 29
Spain / Spanish 4, 5, 6, 8, 9, 10, 11, 13, 16, 19, 21, 32, 33, 35, 38, 39, 42
St Croix River 4, 40
St Lawrence River 40
Stuyvesant, Peter 24, 25
Swedish 24, 25

Talon, Jean-Baptiste 41
Teach, Edward 17
Tennessee 35
Texas 26
Thirteen Colonies 5, 22, 28, 32, 44, 45
Thomson, Charles 34
Tortuga 16
Transatlantic trade 20
Treaty of Aix-la-Chapelle 42
Treaty of Breda 19
Treaty of Paris 28, 35, 44, 45
Treaty of Utrecht 42
Trenton, New Jersey 32
Tupac Amaru 5, 13

United States 4, 32, 34

Valley Forge 32

Valley of Mexico 4
Vela, Blasco Núñez 10
Venezuela 18
Veracruz 9
Vermont 35
Viceroyalty of New Granada 5, 13
Viceroyalty of New Spain 4, 9, 13
Viceroyalty of Peru 4, 10, 11, 13, 18
Viceroyalty of Rio de la Plata 5, 13
Ville-Marie 40
Virginia 4,7, 17, 21, 23, 29, 33, 34, 35

Washington, George 32, 35
West India Company 24
West Indies 39
West, Benjamin 44
Willemstad, Curacao 38
William of Orange 41
Williamsburg, Virginia 39
Wilmington 25
Wolfe, James, General 44

Yorktown 35